Mai Cheng

麦城

Also by Mai Cheng

麦城诗集
  (Selected Verse of Mai Cheng)
词悬浮
  (Verbal Mag-Lev)

Mai Cheng

麦城诗选

Selected Poems

Translated by Denis Mair

Shearsman Books
Exeter

Published in the United Kingdom in 2008 by
Shearsman Books Ltd
58 Velwell Road
Exeter EX4 4LD

www.shearsman.com

ISBN 978-1-905700-88-2

Original poems copyright © Wang Qiang, 1985-2008.
Translations copyright © Denis Mair, 2008.

The right of Wang Qiang (writing as Mai Cheng) to be identified as the author of this work, and of Denis Mair to be identified as the translator thereof, has been asserted by them in accordance with the Copyrights, Designs and Patents Act of 1988. All rights reserved.

Cover: *Desert Forms 2* (Studio still life. Photo-based mixed-medium image) by Elena Ray. Image copyright © Elena Ray, 2006.

Acknowledgements
We are grateful to Jonathan Waley for his translation of the three commentaries on the back cover.

Contents

在一次写作里碰上晓渡和芒克的身影	10
In the Act of Writing, I Meet with the Silhouettes of Tang Xiaodu and Mang Ke	11
信	12
Letter	13
撤出来的词	14
Words Of Withdrawal	15
祭祀	16
Offering To The Dead	17
夜，让我这样说	18
Night, Let Me Put it This Way	19
梦里的蚂蚁	20
Ants in a Dream	21
倾向上的一种练习	22
An Exercise in Tendencies	23
水使我流露	24
An Outpouring Allowed by Water	25
找死	26
Looking for Death	27
废墟里的钟表	28
Clock in the Ruins	29
缝纫机	30
Sewing Machine	31
形而上学的上游	32
Upstream of Metaphysics	33
谁最先知道飞	44
Who First Knows of Flying	45
一枚树叶	48
A Tree Leaf	49
梦呓	50
Dream Babble	51
跟随一列火车到达的冬天	52
Winter Arrived at by Following A Train	53
一封书信	54
Letter from a Friend	55

梦过来以后	56
After a Dream Passes Over	57
彼与此	60
Each and Other	61
磨刀师傅	62
The Master Sharpener	63
南方木匠的北方经历	64
The Northern Experience of a Southern Carpenter	65
油画里的十面埋伏	68
Ambush on All Sides, Painted in Oil	69
梦的里边	70
Inside a Dream	71
正月的下面	74
The Underside of the First Month	75
语言上的危险旅行	76
A Dangerous Trek Across Language	77
失题之八	78
Title Mislaid #8	79
对一面镜子的追问	80
Questioning a Mirror	81
与牙疼有关的一次写作	84
Writing Behind a Toothache	85
纸灯笼里的纸光芒	86
Paper-Softened Beams from a Paper Lantern	87
碎	88
In Pieces	89
原来	90
Back Then	91
本真	92
Core Identity	93
一年来的借	94
A Year's Worth of Borrowing	95
路过医学院门口的一次写作	98
Written While Passing the Gate of a Medical School	99
抽屉里的写作	100
Writings in a Drawer	101
力量	102
Power	103

必须	106
Need	107
鱼	108
A Fish	109
布艺	110
Needlecraft	111
直觉场	112
Intuitive Field	113
今夜，上演悲伤	114
This Evening's Feature Will Be Sorrow	115
桌子上的内心活动	118
Inner Life at the Table	119
麦城：一九八八年孤独成果	122
Mai Cheng's Solitary Achievements of 1988	123
视觉广场	128
The Plaza of Eyesight	129
在困惑里接待生活	132
In Bewilderment, Playing the Host to Life	133
歌剧里的圈套	138
An Operatic Intrigue	139

麦城诗选

Mai Cheng: Selected Poems

在一次写作里碰上晓渡和芒克的身影

一封远方来信
这样写道
他在未来
订了三种世外桃源生活
约我
晓渡、芒克
乘坐陕北民歌
尽快赶到那里去
朦胧诗负责接站

如此美好的约定
被晚餐的筷子
从词语里夹了出来
轻轻地
搁在未来前一天夜里的盘子上
我拿起电话
拨通了跟他俩有关的
两种不同的写作策略
他俩彼此的友情刚刚升位

晓渡说
他只能在未来呆一个上午
他欠生活里最主要的一个夜晚
还没还上
而芒克却是另一种答复
谁也不欠我
我只欠有深度的生活
和北京口音
没说出来的快乐

2004年3月20日

In the Act of Writing, I Meet with the Silhouettes of Tang Xiaodu and Mang Ke

His letter from far away
Had this to say
He had placed an order in the future
For three kinds of life in Shangri-la
He invited me
With Xiaodu and Mang Ke
To hurry there as soon as possible
Riding on a folk song from North Shanxi
Misty Poetry would meet us at the station

Such a lovely invitation
Was plucked from an exchange of words
By the chopsticks of our dinner
And lightly placed on our evening plates
One day before the future
I picked up a telephone
Dialed two strategies of writing
That pertain to the two of them
Whose friendship has recently been promoted

Tang Xiaodu said
He can only spend one morning in the future
He owes life its most important evening
It is time to pay up
But Mang Ke has a different answer
Nobody owes me
I owe something to a life of depth
And to the happiness a Beijing accent
Has not yet uttered

2004/3/20

信
——致晓渡

这封信一打开
晓渡便从纸上
把芒克还给他的思考
递给我
最后，他写道
兄弟，我在下游等你
我朝向墙上的地图
查找他寄过来的那个下游

一面图纸里升起来的船帆
挡住了江南后面的绿
长江的潮水顺着纸上河道
涌向了我
我赶紧借来抽水机
向外排着倒灌在写作里的积水
这时，晓渡打来电话
问我离下游还有多远
我气喘吁吁地回答
下游？是不是我说的那个上游

２００４年３月２１日

Letter
   —for Xiaodu

No sooner had I opened the letter
Than from the paper's surface Tang Xiaodu
Handed me the deep thinking
Mang Ke had restored to him
At the letter's end he wrote
Brother, I will wait for you downstream
I turned to the map on the wall
Sought the downstream he was sending me

A sail unfurled on a sheet of drawing paper
Blocks a green view of river country
The Yangzi tidewaters surge toward me
Along a riverbed on paper
I quickly borrow a pump to expel
The reflux of excess water in my writing
At this moment, Xiaodu rings me up
Asks how long before I reach downstream
In panting breaths I answer
Downstream? Is that what I mean by *upstream?*

2004/3/21

撒出来的词
——为国坤兄思古追旧而作

接着，你向后撤去
撤到一面旧旧的铜镜里
谁的结局跟上了你的撒退
再撒，就到阿房宫啦
可宫里的生活
早已被电影借到了宫外

铜镜里的唐三彩
帮你联系上了你早期的视野
你拿武家的策略
用长途电话折旧着我们和古人的分离
你说，把光芒拿过来
我就能让你看到故乡

故乡？何为故乡
一只快要死去的鸟
让你的表达飞了起来
故乡，就是祖先
反扣在你命运里的一张底牌
故乡：在别处

天安大厦的电梯
把你古色古香的经历
带到了历史的上方
油漆替墙壁
对你的表情
一遍一遍地做着减法

你终于挥舞起
武家的最后一种刀法
砍着从铜镜里
窜出来的历史火苗
火，越烧越大
刀，越舞越美

2004年1月30日

Words of Withdrawal
— for Guokun, and his fascination with antiquity

And so you turn away, withdraw
Pulling back to an old mirror of bronze
Where someone's downfall catches up to you
Pull back further, to E-Fang Palace
But daily life in the palace
Was borrowed for movies outside its walls

The mirror showed Tang figurines in three-color glaze
They helped you connect with your early vision
You used military tactics, made long-distance calls
To depreciate our separation from the ancients
You said, bring on the flashes of brilliance
I will let you see our native ground

Native ground? What would that be?
A bird at the point of dying
Enables your flights of expression
Native ground, which is ancestry
Is a face-down card, buttoned inside your fate
Native ground—is somewhere else

The elevator in the Skyscraper of Heavenly Peace
Lifts your beautifully weathered experience
Into the upper stories of history
Again and again the paint,
In place of the wall, performs subtraction
On your smile or frown

In the end you set dancing
The final moves of a warrior's sword
Slashing at history's tongues of flame
That dart out from a mirror of bronze
The fire burns hotter every moment
Your swordsmanship more beautiful

2004/1/30

祭祀
——献给我的外公和外婆

外公，在坟墓里
校对着碑文
我在坟的外头
点人间的香火

瘦瘦的身躯
瘦瘦的面容
瘦瘦的行程
瘦瘦的影子

从里到外，外公
被瘦归拢在一起
瘦，是他
唯一能留下来的东西

外公的最后一个梦想
准备回传给迷恋故乡的一个背影
却被生死离别
铲出了界外

我拧开酒瓶塞
贴着外公的瘦
对着他内心的空瓶
倒，我的孤独

2004年2月27日

Offering to the Dead
—for my maternal grandparents

My grandfather, inside his grave
Proofreads his burial inscription
While I, outside the grave
Light the incense of the living

Gaunt physique
Gaunt features
Gaunt journey
Gaunt shadow

From inside out, gauntness
Made up my grandfather's very being
Thinness
Was his sole legacy

Grandfather's last dream was supposed to pass on
To a lone shape enamored of our native ground
But the gulf between dead and living
Shoveled it out of the picture

I uncork a wine bottle
Press myself against Grandfather's thinness
Into the empty bottle of his heart
Pouring, my solitude

2004/2/27

夜,让我这样说
——为于立新小妹而作

谁的阴影
踩住了你的脚
下一步
是谁的深渊

你的身子
能不能转过来
转和不转
是我们的什么

我低下生活的态度
跟姜健说
赵野身影的后来
就是我们的江湖

道路用吉普车的轮印
快速抵达我们的内心
我跟芒克说
过来,是另一种回去

2004年2月3日

Night, Let Me Put it This Way
 —*for Miss Yu Lixin*

Whose shadow
Has tread upon your foot
And to whose abyss
Belongs the next footstep?

Can your body
Manage to turn about?
Between turning and not turning
What is chalked up to us?

My low profile of living
Said to a man named Jiang Jian
The aftermath of Zhao Ye's receding form
Will become our underworld

The road arrives quickly in our inner heart
With the wheel treads of a jeep
As I put it to Mang Ke
Passing over is another way of going home

2004/2/3

梦里的蚂蚁

一只蚂蚁
正啃着我梦里的副食
幻想是刚从愿望的笼屉里
蒸出来的灌汤包
幻想里的汤汁和馅
被另一批获得爬行资格的小蚂蚁
吃了个精光

此时此刻
我必须腾出一只手的力量
控制住原有的一切里
刚刚爬进来的新的一切
或者用旧梦对我的许诺
把新梦垫起来
使梦本身
高过蚂蚁的野心
两倍到三倍

梦高起来以后
蚂蚁在地上
反复地演算着
它无法到达的高度

2004年3月21日

Ants in a Dream

A single ant
Nibbles at side dishes in my dream
Fantasy is a plate of juicy dumplings
Fresh from the steaming rack
The stuffing and juice of fantasy
Get eaten by another group of ants
Who have gotten credentials to crawl

At this moment
I must free up the strength of one hand
To control everything new that has crawled
Into the everything that I once knew
Or perhaps pile an old dream's promise
Underneath my new dream
So the dream itself
Can be taller than ants
At least double or triple

Once the dream is raised high
Ants on the ground
Repeatedly work out their figures
Of a height they cannot reach

2004/3/21

倾向上的一种练习

我还是喜欢
一边品尝咖啡
一边吸着烟
静听肖邦的钢琴曲

这是著名的《黑键练习曲》*
它强调右手解决黑暗的倾向
手指在黑白键盘上敲来敲去
像似用乐曲来修理一个国家
到另一个国家最后的楼梯

随着一段黑键快板的出现
我看见肖邦在一个
被黑键敲黑的小夜曲里
往法国搬着自己的波兰国籍
他的左心室却跳动着另一个祖国之谜

练习曲弹完的时候
乔治·桑坐在琴旁低声道
像肖邦那么美丽的手指
居然也漏掉了这么多好时光

2002年5月27日

* 钢琴练习曲。肖邦作于1830年,
因右手全用黑键而得名。

An Exercise in Tendencies

I still enjoy sipping coffee
While smoking a cigarette
Quietly listening to piano works by Chopin

This is the famous "Etude in White and Black"*
It stresses right-hand tendencies of dealing with darkness
Nimble fingers pound on black and white keys
As if using music to repair the final stairway
From one nation to another nation

Evoked by a few measures in *allegro*
I picture the Chopin of the nocturnes
Pounded to darkness by black keys
His freight of Polish identity is underway to France
Even the atrium of his heart
Beats with the riddle of another motherland

As notes of the etude die away
Georges Sand speaks softly from beside the piano
Even from the lovely fingers of Chopin
So much wonderful time slips away

2002/5/27

---

* *This étude, written by Chopin in 1830, gets its title from the right-hand part, which is played wholly on black keys.*

水使我流露

坐在咖啡厅一角
等一个来自下午以外的结果
结果,在一个盘子的上面
也可能在刚刚送来的
这杯水里

水里还有别的水
杯子里的茶叶
被水泡得软如绸缎
端起杯子
水使我慢慢向你流露
而你却乘着水从杯子里
流出来的速度
向另一个结果
奔去

我问咖啡厅主人
一个下午
人有几种结果
他始终低着头
默不作答
我请他把手张开
掌上除了指纹
和他拿物质时惯用的手法
什么也没有

临近黄昏时
水的全部
已离开水杯
面对空空荡荡的杯子
我才发现
空
里面还有一种空

2003年3月6日

An Outpouring Allowed by Water

Sitting in a cafe corner
Waiting for an outcome the afternoon can't contain
The outcome lies on a plate
Or perhaps in this glass of water
Just placed upon my table

In this water is another kind of water
Tea leaves drenched in the glass
Grow as soft as silk streamers
Now I raise this glass
Water allows my outpouring toward you
But you ride the speed of flowing water
Out of a glass, streaking toward
Another outcome
I ask the cafe owner
How many outcomes
An afternoon can have for someone
His head stays lowered
His silence unbroken
I ask him to open his hand
Aside from whorled markings
And his customary grasp of objects
His hand shows nothing

As twilight draws near
The entirety of water
Has departed from the glass
Looking into the unfilled glass
In its emptiness
There is another emptiness

2003/3/6

找死

上午十点左右
接到一个电话
说一个好朋友
刚刚死掉
死在一起车祸里

放下耳鸣
快速赶到电话里的那个段落
那里空无一人
车祸
已被死亡档案拖走

赶到火葬场，我看见
这里处处摆着死亡
哭声，此起彼伏
你无法知道
谁的哭在负责谁的死

在告别大厅
我的哀伤
被悼词拦住
它问我找谁的死
我说，被车撞死的死

楼上，楼下
东厅，西厅
我怎么也找不着
忽然，身后传来一句话
这个人在找死

2003年2月27日

Looking for Death

At around ten in the morning
I receive a phone call
My good friend has just died
Victim of an auto accident

I put down the squeak in my ear
Hurry to the location in the phone call
Nobody is there
The accident has been towed away
Into a death certificate

I hurry to the crematorium, where I see
Death laid out in every corner
Here and there rise sounds of weeping
I have no way to know
Whose weeping is assigned to whose death

In the lobby of farewells
My grief is intercepted by a eulogy
It asks me whose death I search for
I say, for the death that died in a collision

Upstairs, downstairs
East wing, west wing
Cannot find it anywhere
From behind I hear someone say
That man is looking for death

2003/2/27

废墟里的钟表

房屋由东向西摇晃
接着,又由西晃回来
躺在床上的整个家庭
歪斜得像一个巨大的滑梯

恐惧松开道德与伦理
以及爱和被爱
老人和孩子
沿着悲剧的坡度
从人生掉了下去

灾难,是地震
一个一个抱过来的
灾难戴着黑手套
从城里再搜到乡下
之后,废墟替它留言

埋在瓦砾里的手
无法接住远方的哭声
也无法从黑暗中
把从前的天空扒出来

一个七岁的男孩
抱着从废墟里
捡出来的钟表
没有眼泪地哭着

钟摆,依旧滴答滴答地走着
好像在跟孩子说
谁能利用它的声音
从悲剧的内幕
走出来
哪怕走出来的
会是另一个人

2003年3月2日

Clock in the Ruins

The building rocked from East to West
Then rocked back the other way
The whole family lying in bed
Careened as if on a giant sliding board

Fear unstrung their morals and ethics
Their loving and their being loved
Old and young alike
Along the slope of tragedy
Slid out of human life

Disasters in the form of earthquakes
Scooping people up in their embrace
Disasters wearing black gloves
Ransacking from the city to the country
Leaving messages in the form of ruins

Hands buried under broken tiles
Unable to reach distant weeping
Unable in the darkness to unearth
Even a patch of yesterday's sky

A man-child of seven
Sobbing without tears
Holds a clock in his arms
That he pulled from the ruins

The clock goes on ticking
As if asking the child
What person will use this sound
To walk out from the curtain
Of this hidden tragedy
Even if the one who walks out
Will be a different person?

2003/3/2

缝纫机

一九六六年
大年初一的前一天
我跟活在皮肤里的姥姥说
把这台缝纫机
卖了吧
换了钱
把节日赎回来

姥姥听后
气哼哼地回答
卖了它
家里这么多的伤心事
如何缝
又如何补

随后
姥姥脚踏上缝纫机
嗒嗒嗒，嗒嗒嗒
她刚刚的那一份表达
随针线一起
织进了我的蓝布衣里

多年以后
放学回家的路上
蓝布衣上的一根线头开了
我顺手一拽
姥姥的那份表达
被我越拽越长

2003年3月12日

Sewing Machine

On the eve of the holiday
The New Year of 1966
I told my grandmother
Who lived in her skin
To sell the sewing machine
With the money it made
Could redeem the holiday

With a *humph* and a *harrumph*
Grandma gave me an answer
Once we sell it
How do we sew
And how do we patch
All our family heartbreaks?

Then with her rhythmic foot
Grandma treadled away
clickety-whirr, clickety-whirr
The expression on her face
Was stitched along with the thread
Into my blue cotton jacket

Years later, coming home after school
A thread came loose on my jacket
Unthinkingly I pulled
Which drew out her expression
Further and further

2003/3/12

形而上学的上游

一
火车轮子
大声盘问着逃进铁里的轨
铁，总是输给车轮

轨道下的枕木
控制着木匠的野心
坐在尾节车厢里的男孩
端起玩具枪
瞄父母离婚的背景

二
你没有多少向往地站着
像看着玻璃电梯里的我
那样地站着
嘴角似乎沾了一个歌词
歌词，正拉拢离你最近的旋律
唱我的孤独

三
天堂的后视镜
把分不开山羊和绵羊的憨翎姐姐
从乡下拽到了城里
山羊在镜子里
啃着城里的百货

四
实验室里的乡音
将远和近递给了物理
水，一定在水流的上游活着
玻璃上的雾气
使窗户把窗外看得格外重

五
祖母和外祖母
脸上的皱褶

Upstream of Metaphysics

1.
Wheels of a train
Loudly interrogate the iron retreat of rails
Iron will always lose to train wheels

Wooden ties beneath the rails
Control a carpenter's ambition
A boy seated in the caboose
Levels his toy gun
At his parents' divorced backs

2.
Standing without much expectation
In a manner of standing
Like watching myself in a glass elevator
Mouth corners twitch with lyrics
Lyrics entice the melody nearest you
To sing of my solitude

3.
The rearview mirror of heaven
Has dragged Sister Gracewing, who can't tell goats from sheep
Out of the country into the city
The goat in the mirror
Chews up city merchandise

4.
The accent in a laboratory
Hands near and far over to physics
Water, upstream of this watery flow must be alive
Fog on a pane of glass
Gives extra heaviness to a window's view outside

5.
Wrinkles on the faces
Of both my grandmothers

被手风琴收起来
敲门声与啄木鸟
混响在一起
空杯坠落,清脆地说
神碎了一地
——在你身后

六

我踮起脚尖
够油画里的那把钥匙
这里那么多的门
没有一扇有锁孔
看来,钥匙也是一种假设

七

几个线条
就把狗的忠诚
逼得离你这么近
狗。西方的狗
忠诚落到纸上
也是杂色的

狗的目光
刚刚赶到狗的眼睛里
这条狗
便从画的技法里
蹿了出去

傍晚,狗叼着一块
被肉抛弃已久的骨头
向画的深处走去

八

戴上手套
用手套上的手指
一层层地揭开亲人的伤痕
你捂住双耳
掩盖着来自身体左侧的哭

Closed up with an accordion
Door knock and woodpecker
Mingle their sounds
Fall of empty glass, words crisply spoken
God is in pieces on the floor—
There behind you

6.
I rise up on tiptoe
Reach for a key in a painting
So many doors in this place
Not one with a keyhole
The key too must be a supposition

7.
Just a few painted lines
Press the loyalty of a dog
Right up against you
Doggishness. The loyalty of Western dogs
When rendered on paper
Has those same mongrel spots

A thoughtful gaze
No sooner finds its way to the dog's eyes
Than this brushwork dog in the painting
Dashes away

It runs deep into the painting at twilight
Clamping a bone in its jaws
That was rejected by meat

8.
Put on a pair of gloves
Use the fingers of the glove
To peel back layers of a loved one's scar
Cup hands over your ears
Cover up the sobbing on your body's left side

九

盘子端过来的时候
我正好从筷子上
往田间走
盘子越来越接近盘子的事实
它呆在南方的菜谱里
看，谁最先娶走胃口
你的挑来挑去
从自己开始
再由自己结束

十

药方领着病情
赶到了乡村邮局
寄我牙齿上的疼
邮票，贴在往事的右上角
请于下周二
查看你的邮箱

十一

乌云、高尔基的大胡子
暴风雨比他的外套
来得还要早
小说里的核心人物
端着乡愁的木碗

谁最先浮出水面
谁就先拥有上游

十二

童年，就是一枚绿扣子
从鞋帮
往上钉
一直钉到领口

十三

一个词
惊动了一个人的写作动机
也惊动了人间的香火
所谓的文学虚构

9.
As plates are carried to the table
I take the path of a chopstick
Into the fields
The plate gets closer to the plate's facticity
It bides time in a southern recipe
Let's see who's first to marry appetite
Your way of picking at morsels
Begins with you
And ends with you

10.
A prescription leads a condition by the arm
Into a village post office
To send off the pain in my teeth
Stamp glued to upper right of times gone by
Next Tuesday please check for it
In your mailbox

11.
Dark clouds, Gorky's beard
The storm arriving
Ahead of his overcoat
Protagonist in a novel
Bearing a homesick wooden bowl
The one who first floats to the surface
Is the one who owns the headwaters

12.
Childhood is a green hook
From the side of my shoe
Piercing all the way up
To an eyelet in my collar

13.
A single phrase
Sets his motive for writing in an uproar
And stirs up new offerings of incense
The so-called construct of literature

被踢翻在地
隐喻和反隐喻
划了两道长长的口子
血,从另一个人的阅读里
向外地流

十四
一则广告
贴在小区的楼道里
本人,管道工
具二十余年工作经验
专修暖气阀门
和疏通上下水管道
如需要,亦可
疏通各种社会关系
并负责权力的安装
调试和维修
联系方式
列宁在一九一八

十五
清明节
去郊外墓地
我的哀思和埋在这里的
一个人的尊严
于十点一刻
秘密接头
尊严在高处
我慢慢向上走
在第十二个台阶下
不慎滑倒
倒下去的姿势,好像
与埋在深处的死亡
重叠在了一起
我抬了一下眼睛,发现
我的影子还呆在原处

十六
骰子共有六面
六面绝不是机遇的六种

Kicked over on the ground
Metaphors and counter-metaphors
Have dug two long gouges
Blood, by way of someone's reading
Trickles toward outer regions

14.
Advertising flier
Pasted in the stairway of a sub-complex
Pipe-fitter at your service
Over twenty years on the job
With a specialty in heating ducts
Skilled at clearing upward and downward pipes
If needed, I can also
Clear up your social channels
And take charge of power installation
Adjustments and repairs made
In your mode of making connections
See Lenin, in 1918

15.
On Tomb Sweeping Day
A graveyard on the outskirts
As morning nears noon
My grieving thoughts
Get together in secret
With the dignity of a buried soul
The dignity is in a high place
I slowly ascend
On the twelfth step I slip
And my tumbling form
Appears superimposed on death
That is buried deep below
I raise my eyes and discover
My shadow has not moved

16.
A die has six sides
Surely not six kinds of probability

四个人
隶属东西南北四个风向
发财的"發"字
蹲在幺鸡的身后
鼓捣它把游戏里的财富
叼过来
喂你当下的命运
那个矮胖子
不停地摇晃着手心里的骰子
他身后的阿拉伯表哥说
运气，摇是摇不出来的

我第一手抓来的牌
是一对西风
第二手
是个南风
第三手牌抓起来一看
竟又是个北风
还未等我看到东风
窗外树上的叶子
已落满街道

　　　　十七
铁轨
从毛泽东时代的夜色里
铺过来之后
一个人影
和他的前程
开始交付使用
忧郁倚靠着火车的时速惯性
哀求着悲伤
在下一个山谷
减速

　　　　十八
车站扳道工身后的那个
乡村孩子
目睹了扳道岔的全过程
他的好奇
与道岔的移动

Four persons correspond
To winds of the four directions—north, east, south, west
The word "rich" crouches
Behind a plumed female
And nudges her to bring you
The luck of the game in her beak
Which she'll stuff in the maw of your momentary fate
A short, fat man
Keeps shaking the dice in his hand
His Arab cousin behind him says
Luck does not come by shaking

The first tiles I draw
Are a pair of west winds
On my second draw
I get a south wind
I turn up my third draw
Wouldn't you know—a north wind
Before I can see the east wind
Leaves from the tree at the window
Have fallen all over the street

17.
Since iron rails
From the dark night of the Mao Zedong era
Were laid all the way here
A man's shadow
And his prospects
Have to be used in alternation
Dread depends on the train's momentum
But it pleads with sorrow
Going into another valley
To reduce its speed

18.
Behind the railroad switchman
A village child witnesses
The operation of switching tracks
The tripping of the switch
Gets wholly absorbed

合并在了一起
他暗暗自语
什么时候
他八岁的向往
能被扳道工
从这一边扳到另一边

另一边，是哪一边？

２００４年３月２０日

Into his curiosity
And he asks himself
When can his eight-year-old wishes
Be switched by the switchman
From this side to another?

That other track, where would it lead?

2004/3/20

谁最先知道飞
——为继海弟回国参加世界杯而作

四月二十八日,一只英国鸟
在飞里
看见了他手里攥着的机票上飞着的飞
随轮子离地的一刹那
他将被一个句子带回祖国

谁　最先知道飞

在机场的柜台
英国小姐
安排他坐在飞的第一排
他恳求能否坐在翅膀的位置上
这样,他将有两种飞
一块飞,或飞中飞

谁　最先知道飞

透过候机大厅的玻璃
他一眼看见了
停在跑道上
即将起飞的中国领土
他突然明白了
他将要进行的是飞来飞去的飞
而不是飞走的飞

谁　最先知道飞

坐在飞起来的名单里
他端起一杯热茶
喝下了他想要喝下去的一切
他知道十几天后
一些日子也会飞起来
国家的领土将和足球一样大
有许许多多的景色和脸色
将被他悄悄地种植在
体育的右下方

Who is First to Know of Flight
—for Ji Haidi's return to China, to play in the World Cup

April 28, a bird from England
Already in flight, saw another chance to fly
Take wing in the ticket he was holding
As wheels leave the ground he will be carried off
By a few simple words to his homeland

Who is first to know of flight?

At the airport counter
A young British miss
Books him a seat in the first row of flight
He requests a seat overlooking a wing
This way, two ways of flying will be in flight
At once, or call it flight within flying

Through the waiting area window
At a glance he can recognize
Out on the tarmac
A piece of Chinese territory poised for flight
Right then he knows he is destined for
The flight that flies back and forth
Not flight that flies away

Who is first to know of flight?

Now that he is seated on the flight list
He raises a cup of tea
Drinks what he wishes to drink
Looking forward to two weeks later
When a few special days will take flight
His country's borders will grow as wide as soccer
And deft movements of his feet
Will place key plays and replays
In an unblockable corner of fandom

谁　最先知道飞

飞机离北京越来越近
他在座位上睡着了
从飞里转移到梦里
继续飞
飞着飞着
一只鸽子跟他说
请把笼子拆掉
我让你看见
和平里面的飞
一条餐桌上的鱼说
请把我放回到原处
我让你看见
在谁的水里我都能飞
一片落下来的秋叶跟他说
请把大地打扫干净
我让你看见
在树的根须里面的飞
国坤的女儿宝宝说
继海叔叔，我就快看见你在足球里面的飞啦
叔叔，你还有别的飞吗

谁　最先知道飞

2002年5月10

Who is first to know of flight?

The plane gets closer to Beijing
He falls asleep in his seat
Shifts from flight to dreaming
And continues flying
As he flies along
A dove says to him
Please dismantle my cage
I will let you see
Peace in flight
A fish on a banquet table says
Please put me back where I belong
And you will see how I can fly
In any territorial waters
A fallen leaf says to him
Please sweep the good earth clean
Someday you will even see
Flight in the rootlets of a tree
Guokun's daughter Baobao says
Uncle Jihai, soon I will see you in flight
Within the game of soccer
Uncle, do you fly in other ways?

Who is first to know of flight?

2002/5/10

一枚树叶

一枚秋天的树叶
落在地上
我弯腰捡起它
随手夹在一本书里

树叶的名字
我说不出来
它的形状
很像住在我目光上的
一个人的眼睛

回到家里
外面刮起阵阵大风
此时我看见
许多手正使劲地拽着玻璃
摇晃着我的经历

刚刚坐定下来
家里突然也有风吹叶动的声音
顺着声音寻去
原来那片被夹着的树叶
在书里刮起了风

这突如其来的一切
吓得我冷汗淋淋
我担心这捡回来的风声
会不会和外面的风拧成风暴

2003. 2. 21

A Tree Leaf

Leaf of an autumn tree
Falls to the ground
I bend to pick it up
Press it in pages of a book

The name of this leaf
I cannot recognize
Its shape resembles
A person's eye
As my gaze sweeps by

When I return home
I see gusts of wind in hands
Brushing roughly at the window
Tossed about like my experience

Once I've settled in my seat
Even indoors there is a whisper of leaves
When followed to its source the sound
Turns out to come from that pressed leaf
Stirring a wind between the pages

All of this coming so suddenly
Frightens me into a cold sweat
What if the wind sounds I brought home
Twist together with outdoor winds
Into a storm?

2003/2/21

梦呓

恶梦死死摁住我的手
并从指纹里
一点点掏空我仅存的隐私
智力，被罚在另一个恶梦里站着
我无力让尊严翻过身来
双腿的力量
被一条小路占用至今
那些被胶水粘住的话语
没扯出多远
就被恶梦的影子扑倒在地
后来，我整个儿
被恶梦摁进土里
黑暗中我看见一个农民
他说他是和种子一起种进来的
我问他
我们什么时候能够长出去
他回答
从死亡长出来的东西
活也活不长久
然后我们沉默。然后他反问
什么叫"入土为安"

2003年2月23日

Dream Babble

The nightmare's death-grip takes my hand
Empties my fingerprints of their final secrets
My intellect, made to stand in a horrific corner
Lacks strength to set my dignity upright
The strength of my legs
Has been taken over by a little road
My words stuck together with glue
Hardly begin to digress
Before shadows lay them low
My whole length goes down
Hag-ridden into the dirt by nightmares
In the darkness I see a peasant
Planted down here among the seeds
I ask him when
We can grow above the soil
He says to me
Things that grow out of death
Won't be alive for very long
We grow silent; it is his turn to ask
What does it mean to say
"Interred and at rest"?

2003/2/23

跟随一列火车到达的冬天
——致文康兄

冬天蹲在报纸的一条广告里
乘务员给你倒水时
雪花从报纸的最后一个形容词里
慢慢地飘散开去

雪花的花朵
愈开愈大
你不得不站起来
把这张报纸的一个栏目
卷成明清两代花瓶
插进双倍的冬天

火车由南向北行驶
你热爱的东西
却是由北向南
这时,你给我发来一条短信
即使截住了这列火车
也无法截住和火车一样快的这首诗歌

火车在沈阳停下来
你在前,真理的替身在后
它引导你走进冬天
站台上接你的只有一个小雪人
雪人的嘴满是冰茬
说不出更多的话温暖你

从大连到沈阳四百多公里
但你我的距离
已被车上的南方木匠
卷进他那把卷尺里
他说,那个距离
他永远也无法从卷尺里拉出来

汽笛鸣的一声
冬天又向别的地方开去

Winter Arrived at by Following a Train
— for Wenkang, my brother

Winter hunkers down in newspaper advertisements
As the train attendant fills your tea glass
Snowflakes drift slowly down
From the last glowing phrase

The six-petalled snowflakes
Bloom in greater and greater profusion
You can't help getting to your feet
Roll up a headline story like a pair of vases
One from the Ming, one from the Qing
Which you will insert into this double winter

The train runs from south to north
But the things you love
Head from north to south
At this point you send me a letter
Even if you could hold back this train
You cannot hold this poem as fast as a train

The train stops at Shenyang
You walk in front, the scapegoat of truth walks behind
And guides you in the direction of winter
Only a snowman is on the platform to meet you
The snowman's mouth is full of icicles
He cannot say much to warm your heart

From Dalian to Shenyang is 400 kilometers
But the distance between us
Has been rolled into a tape measure
By the southern carpenter who rides with you
He says that distance
Can never be unrolled
From his measuring tape

The steam whistle wails
Winter heads off to other places

一封书信
——为吴俊兄而作

你来信说
此时，南方阴雨连绵
我看得出来
信中的每一个比喻
都撑着一把雨伞

你反复提到南方的好时光
你说，近日将派一首歌曲前往北方
绕过中学时代的语文
绕开两个人的内心活动
把好时光的由来带给我

我转过身
朝向墙上的地图
仔细地掐算
好时光需几天
才能从地图里走出来

地图上的一些界标
已被磨损得模模糊糊
我怎么也看不清楚
行走在纸上
好时光的影子

黄昏时
我听见急促的敲门声
推开门
南方好时光
已站在我的门口

我端出两把椅子
一把给它
另一把留给美学
而好时光却坐在了
一杯酒的岸边

Letter from a Friend
—for Wu Jun, my brother

You write from the South to tell me
Gloomy days of rain stretch endlessly
That is plain to see
Even the metaphors in your letter
Are carrying umbrellas

You persist in mentioning good times down South
You say you'll soon dispatch a song up north
Making a detour around high school grammar
Around two people's inner vicissitudes
It will deliver to me the source of good times

I turn to the map on the wall
Carefully count on my fingers
How many days the good times need
Before they walk down from the map

Some boundary markers on the map
Are worn and indistinct
However I search for good times
No clear trace appears
Moving across the paper

At the twilight hour
I hear an urgent knock
Push the door open
And good times from the South
Are standing in my doorway

I bring out two more chairs
One for good times
The other for aesthetics
But good times take a seat
On the bank of a wineglass

梦过来以后

梦把我接到城里
废电池交代出的那道目光
使我看到了
另一个故乡的轮廓
道路右侧的沉默
说服着道路左侧的沉默
这是路灯下达的命令

玻璃电梯
慢慢向上抬高我的身份
跟在身份后面的那个婚姻
被港台歌曲
装在进口的旋律里
让邓丽君的演唱方式
从外地唱到内地

我坐在玻璃屏幕
最反光的那一部分里
看财富出入时的举止
窗外的灯红酒绿
劫走我的目光
目光里
还有别的目光

少女的红色短裙
将蹲在她肤色里的男人心态
烘烤得裂开了一条缝
调酒师如此均匀地
把酒色勾兑在一个杯子里
女人给男人倒酒
男人的醉意往女人的深处跳

在夜色扎堆的地方
新黑暗搂着旧黑暗
梦，促使我换了一套新的出身
皮鞋、领带、风衣

After a Dream Passes Over

A dream paved my way to the city
A glimpse provided by a surge
From an out-of-date battery
Showed a different view of my native ground
The silence on the left side of the road
Persuaded the silence on the right
By order of the street light

A glass elevator
Slowly lifted my social standing
And the marriage that fell in line behind it
Was bottled by pop songs from Taiwan
With their imported melodies
As Theresa Teng's singing style
Moved from outer to inner regions

There I was, sitting at the most reflective part
Of a transparent screen
Watching mannerisms of wealth enter and leave
My gaze was hijacked
By lurid signs winking through glass
But behind that gaze
Was yet another gaze

A teenager's red mini-skirt
Scorched by toughness under her skin
Opens a split at the seam
The bartender measures precisely
Two densities of liquor in a glass
A woman pours liquor for a man
His spinning head leaps toward her recesses

In places where nightfall lies in heaps
New darkness embraces old darkness
Spurred by the dream, I try on a new status
Leather shoes, neckties, trench coat

我像一盏被关掉
又重新拧亮的灯
追赶着另一盏灯里的光

十字路口的红绿灯
拦截住我的梦
以及梦境里的另一个我
我试着动用眼前的这一笔绵绵夜色
垫高我今夜的品质
然后，从报废的经历峡谷里
跳过去

去，还是不去
梦过来以后

2004年3月11日

Like a turned-off lamp
Turned on once again
I hurry after another lamp's light

At a crossing the signal light
Brings my dream to a halt
Along with the self that rambled in dreams
Now night-blue air stretches before me
I try to use it, to elevate the night to higher quality
Then, over the canyon of discarded experience
To make the leap

To go or not to go?
After the dream passes over

2004/3/11

彼与此

石匠
捡起地上的一块石头
远远地扔了出去
石头越过一座大山
在大山的后面
重重地落了下去
石匠
翻过山脉后
落地的石头
已变成了另一座大山
石匠莫名其妙
明明扔出去的是一块石头
转眼之间
怎么变成了大山

回到村子
他把疑惑讲给乡亲们听
男女老少纷纷替他猜解
大山是什么?
大山就是石头里的石头
你是什么?
你就是我里面的他
我是什么?
我就是他里面的我们
我们是什么?
我们就是人间的石头

２００４年３月５日

Each and Other

A stonemason
Picks up a stone on the ground
Throws it as far as he can
The stone arcs over a mountain
Falls heavily to earth
The stonemason
Crosses over a ridgeline
To where the fallen stone
Has become another mountain
On the other side
The stonemason is puzzled
What he threw was plainly a stone
How could it turn into a mountain
In the blink of an eye?

Back in the village
He tells the village folk of his bewilderment
Men, women, old and young, offer a slew of guesses
What is a mountain anyway
But the stone within a stone?
And what is a *you*
But the *he* within the "I"?
And what is an "I"
But the *we* within the *he*?
And what are we
But a stone within humanity?

2004/3/5

磨刀师傅

他把刀刃
冲向磨石
上下来回地摩擦
磨着 磨着
那把刀不见了
但他还是低着头
在磨石上蹭来蹭去
直到一道光
磨进了我的眼里
他才抬起头
看了看我

这时，来磨刀的人
越来越多
磨刀师傅把要磨到的一切
排了排队
洒上一点水
随后又开始进入
那貌似单调的工作程序

当他把磨好的刀递给他们时
我发现
在隐隐跳动的额纹下
他的目光
比刀锋还快

2003年2月26日

The Master Sharpener

He holds the knife's edge
Against the whetstone
Grinding this way and that
Grinding and grinding some more
Now the blade disappears
With head still lowered
He makes passes over the whetstone
Until a glint of steel
Whets itself against my eyes
Then he lifts his head
Levels his gaze at me

By this time, more and more people
Are coming to sharpen their knives
The master lines up everything
That is due to be sharpened
He sprinkles a few drops of water
Then buckles down to his regimen
Of work that appears monotonous

As he hands them the whetted knives
I discover
Beneath the tremor of his creased brow
The look in his eyes
Is sharper than knives

2003/2/26

南方木匠的北方经历

他的手指
竖起
是一排树林
放平
是一根根好木头

他的爷爷
从明朝返回
用指纹
替他复印了一套
老祖宗的手艺

他打的第一件家具
是一扇雕花的门
油漆刷好之后的第三天
他慢慢拧开门把手
走进了北方

他打的第二件家具
是一张大木床
就这样，一场双人梦
任由红松木
硬拼在了一起

他打的第三个家具
是一个工艺精美的衣橱
从柜子里
拿出来的形象
从不会沾半点灰尘

为了一个不停地在他面前
晃来晃去的老太太的身影
他决定打一把椅子
他的信念是一旦椅子打好
他就能认出那身影

The Northern Experience
of a Southern Carpenter

Standing up
His fingers
Were a grove of trees
Lying flat
Columns of fine wood

His grandfather
Having returned from the Ming dynasty
Left him a set
Reproduced with fingerprints
Of ancestral craftsmanship

The first piece of furniture he built
Was a carved wooden door
On the third day, having brushed on lacquer
He slowly turned the latch
Walked into the North

The second piece of furniture he built
Was a large frame bed
And so it happened, that a dream for two
Let itself be clamped together
On a frame of red pinewood

The third piece of furniture he built
Was an exquisite armoire
The image-enhancing clothes
Pulled out from this armoire
Had never known a speck of dust

For the fitful shape of an old woman
That hovered in front of him
He decided to make a chair
Believing that the chair, once made
Would let him recognize her shape

椅子做好之后
晃动的身影却突然停止了晃动
他肩扛着椅子
走遍北方去寻找那身影
他甚至把好几个冬天都翻了个

这以后,南方木匠
再没打过一个家具
开始时,是他陪着椅子
到后来,是椅子陪着他
就那么一直站着,在北方

2003年2月27日

Once the chair was made
The fitful shadow stopped flitting
He shouldered the chair
Seeking her shape throughout the North
He even turned some winters upside down

From then on the southern carpenter
Never made furniture again
At first, he kept that chair company
Later, the chair kept him company
In this way he kept standing, in the North

2003/2/27

油画里的十面埋伏

这幅画
出自一名家之手
他用最上等的色彩
涂抹画布上少女的内心活动

少女怀抱着一把琵琶
坐在旧社会的顶层
她演奏的那支曲子
好像刚刚从秦朝传过来

台下只有一位听众
这是一个复辟成性的军阀
他把枪管当成烟斗
嘴角，硝烟滚滚

曲子弹到最后
从少女的琴弦上，跳下来一个
手持匕首的北方刺客
军阀慌忙投奔项羽麾下

面对这幅油画
我多想画家把少女的年龄画给我
最好把她生与死的意境
也画给我

2003.2.2

Ambush on All Sides, Painted in Oil

In this oil painting
From the hand of a noted master
His matchless palette renders the inner mood
Of the girl portrayed on canvas

The girl cradles a *pipa* in her arms
Sits at the peak of traditional society
The piece she performs
May have come down from the Qin

An audience of one before the stage
Is a warlord, reactionary to the bone
He smokes through a rifle barrel
Gun smoke puffs from his mouth

As she plays the composition to the end
Down from the girl's *pipa* strings
Jumps a knife-wielding northern assassin
The warlord flees for refuge under Xiang Yu's flag*

Facing this painting I think
If only the artist could impart the girl's youthfulness
Or better yet, how she senses her own mortality
In the medium of painting

2003/2/2

---

* *Xiang Yu was a contender in the internecine fighting after the fall of the Qin. He overthrew the First Qin Emperor, but failed to win popular support. He was ultimately defeated by the founder of the Han dynasty.*

梦的里边

来自江南的晚上十点
她登上夜光这支梯子
爬进我的梦里
紧接着我听见
翻箱倒柜的声音
——它甚至在梦里也发出回声

我问她寻找什么
她说她饿了
我告诉她梦的左侧有半块面包
她说还有没有比半块面包
更完整的情节
我回答道
那个东西
早已被人拿走了
待我抬头看她时
她已在我梦的最里边
躺在了异梦同床的上面

我刚想从梦里迈出来
她又喊住了我
她说她的梦太冷
能否找个东西盖在上面
沉默片刻，我试着把用过的一个美梦
递给她
她比划了半天
说还是短了一点
她的两条腿和面部的忧郁
依旧露在了美梦的外面
我悄声回答道
只有我身影的长度
能把你露在外面的一切遮住
但那是天亮时的事
她听了大笑了起来
笑声如此之大
乃至把我从梦里推了出来

Inside a Dream

From nightfall in Yangzi River country
She mounts a ladder of phosphors
Crawls into my dream
Before long, I hear the noise
Of her ransacking my possessions
In this dream there is an echo effect

I ask what she is after
She says she is hungry
I tell her there is a crust of bread
On the left side of this dream
She asks if the plot contains
More fulfillment than a bread crust
I say that what she refers to
Has been taken by someone else
Upon looking up I find
She has laid down deep in my dream
On a marriage bed of extramarital dreams

I am ready to walk out from my dream
She stops me short with a cry
Tells me her dream is too cold
Maybe we can find something to cover her
I pause, then hand her a used-up fantasy
Let her see if it will fit
She gestures this way and that
To show it won't reach far enough
The anxiety of her legs and face
Stick out from the edge of my fantasy
In a low voice I answer
Only my body has the length
To cover your protruding parts
But daybreak has come by then
She laughs loudly at my words
Such a loud guffaw is sufficient
To push me out of my dream

这时，妻子也推了我一把
并狠狠地说了句
梦是个什么东西

2003年2月9日

Right then, my wife also pushed me
As she icily said these words
What good is a no-account dream?

2003/2/9

正月的下面

正月，北风招来漫天飞雪
做冬天最后一道作业
主人翻弄着暖瓶
跟我嘀咕着春天的口供

我轻轻地用手指
刻划着玻璃上的霜花
想一下子把冷
从你的目光里
刮下来

你用名人的方式
从桥上向桥下走
并习惯地掏出古董式的怀表
盘算着一个人的知名度
在哪一个台阶上停

你走得太慢
桥上的女孩
早已被风吹进了景色
你哪一种仰望
能做她身姿的画框

我拿起桌子上的蜡笔
画着你的晚餐
奶油画在你忧伤的上面
还是糖
画在你痛苦的下面

2004年2月10日

The Underside of the First Month

First month—north wind brings swirling snow
To perform the final operation of winter
The owner fiddles with his thermos jug
Gruffly offers a spring confession

Lightly with my fingers
I draw lines on frosted panes
Wondering how to scrape away
All the coldness of your gaze

In the manner of someone famous
You descend from an overhead bridge
By habit checking your old-fashioned watch
Figuring which step
Your reputation should rest on

Before you take a few slow steps
The girl on the bridge is carried by wind
Far into the scenery
Your lifted gaze
Pictures her dwindling form

I lift a crayon from the table
To paint your dinner
Would you rather I paint butter
Over the sadness above you
Or sugar on the pain beneath you?

2004/2/10

语言上的危险旅行

检察官用本地方言
提审着外省的伤口
疼和痛
紧紧挨着检察官的审问

伤口与六个身影有关
身子早已失踪
影子却成了伤口的胶片
什么是这疑问的底版

伤口抬动了一下
亲人的哀伤
它借审讯和审讯出来的烟雾
交代着南方的另外几块伤疤

天,渐渐暗下来
审讯,却越来越亮
检察官撕开伤口上的伤痕
问,谁是谁的伤口

2004年2月10日

A Dangerous Trek Across Language

A prosecutor employs a local accent
To examine an out-of-state wound
Pain and agony
Lend weight to his questions

The wound relates to six human shapes
Whose bodies are now untraceable
Their shadows have entered into a bandage
What is the underlying puzzle here?

The wound shifts the weight
Of grieving family members
Uses the smoke of questions fired both ways
To disclose more scars from southern places

The heavens gradually darken
But the questioning gets brighter
The prosecutor tears the scar from the injury
Asking who is wounded, who is the wound?

2004/2/10

失题之八

一只鸟的影子
落在小女孩的课本上
外公一声咳嗽
影子吓飞了
小女孩抬头朝向天空
鸟的影子
掠过她的作业

她合上课本
一阵阵鸟鸣
从作业里传出来
外公顿觉好奇
翻开了她的课本
但只闻其声
不见其影

2004年2月25日

Title Mislaid #8

A bird's shadow
Falls on a girl's schoolbook
At the sound of grandfather's cough
The shadow flies away
The girl lifts her head skyward
As the bird's shadow
Skims over her homework

She closes her notebook
But the cries of a bird
Are heard from between the pages
Grandfather, seized by curiosity,
Leafs through the pages
But only hears the sound
Can't see the slightest shadow

2004/2/25

对一面镜子的追问

是头重
还是脚轻
他的脸
刚刚挂上这面镜子里
一转身
就栽了下去

他把镜子
翻过来翻过去
看了好半天
也没看见脸掉在了哪里

于是,他把镜子投向大地
故乡的花
一下子就开了

忽然,一个上学的孩子
跑进这面镜子里
摘下镜子里所有的花朵
说要把这一束束鲜花
带回学校
让老师讲课的声音
四季分明

他低下头
跟随镜子的折光
往内心走
快要走到灵魂深处的时候
这面镜子
突然从墙上掉了下来
（距离他的内心活动
被四分五裂,仅差一个毫米）

他看见
那聪明的孩子
手捧着花
从坠落的镜面跳了出去

QUESTIONING A MIRROR

Was it his heavy head
Or his unsteady feet?
At the moment the mirror was hung
His face turned around
Dropped to the floor

He turned the mirror
This way and that
For a long time he could not find
Where his face had fallen
And so flung the mirror onto this good earth
Before long flowers were blooming
On his native land

Right then a school-age child
Ran into that mirror world
Plucked all the flowers he found there
Said he would take bouquets of flowers
Back with him to school
So the teacher's classroom voice
Could have four distinct seasons

He lowered his head
Followed the mirror's deflected light
Deep into his heart
He had almost reached his soul's core
When the mirror fell
(A centimeter from smashing
  His inner life to smithereens)

He caught a glimpse
Of that clever child
Bouquet in hand
Fleeing the fallen mirror's surface
To land on a slope of native ground
Where the hills and valleys came alive
With blooming wildflowers

落在故乡的山坡上
这时，满山遍野的花
也跟着开了

蹲在地上
他把摔碎的镜片
拼凑在一起
才发现，他的脸
原来也是碎的

2002年5月20日

Squatting on the ground
He pieced together pieces
Of fragmented mirror
Only to discover that his face
Was broken to begin with

2002/05/20

与牙疼有关的一次写作

疼,从牙齿的北方
向牙齿的南方疼去

我躺在医学的备用名单上
药,追上了我的疼
疼拉着痛的手
企图从道德的栏杆上翻过去

医生拿着小锤
在牙齿上
敲过来又敲回去
他要我把疼递给他

大夫,别碰我的地方口音
它们不过是一种路过
医生回答
疼,其实也是一种路过

大约半个钟头
我由病历里站起来
从镜子的上方,我看见
疼,向另一个地址逃去

此时,电话铃声响起
西安沈奇跟我要一个比喻的结果
我沉默不语
担心疼会不会从电话里穿过去

2003年3月14日

Writing Behind a Toothache

Pain, from the north side of my teeth
Aching all the way to dental south
As I lie on the waiting list of medicine
Until a pill catches up to the pain
Pain and agony holding hands, in a pact
To jump over the railing of right and wrong

The dentist with a mallet in hand
Aiming at my tooth
Taps at various angles
Wants me to fork over the pain

Doctor, don't crack my provincial accents
They are only passing by here
But the doctor replies
Pain is another kind of passing by

Half and hour goes by
I stand up from my record chart
And in the airspace over a mirror
Watch pain abscond to a new address

At this point the telephone rings
A friend in Xian wants the result of the metaphor
I do not say a word
But the pain in my heart
Can be felt through the telephone line

2003/03/14

纸灯笼里的纸光芒

姥姥跟我说
她打小的时候
仅用一个纸叠的灯笼
守岁

姥姥拎着它
东家走走，西家看看
凭这盏纸灯笼
想把这么大的节日照在窗户上
或照亮的童年里的疑问
真是难上难

讲着讲着
我忽然看见一个人影
比穆仁智还穆仁智
拎着大红灯笼
从京戏的地方口音里
迈步出来

一个黑暗向另一个黑暗奔去
灯笼里现有的光线
无法照射出一个角色的全部困境
由此，我发现
贫困，不反光

尽管，姥姥叠的那盏灯笼
早已不在
但，纸灯笼里的纸光芒
却还在照着姥姥的脸

2004年2月8日

Paper-Softened Beams from a Paper Lantern

Grandmother told me
When she was little
They had one folded-paper lantern
To bring in the New Year

She dangled it her fingers
Gallivanted through the neighborhood
That lantern's glow at the window
Would light up the whole holiday
Or even shed light on childhood questions
But that was too tall an order

While she was speaking
I saw a human shape
More of a landlord than any landlord
A large red lantern dangling from his hand
Taking stage steps out of the accent
Of an old time opera

One dark patch ran toward another
All the beams a lantern could muster
Could not pierce the shadows
Of a character's predicament

At that point I discovered
That poverty has no surface to catch light

Though it is long-gone
That folded paper lantern
Its paper-softened beams
Still glow on grandmother's face

2004/02/08

碎

深夜一点
在一张旧纸里
我听到一句比旧纸还要旧的话
我走向桌子
贴近那张旧纸
左看，右看
纸里的人没有说话
甚至连说话的爷爷
也没看见
气得我把纸搓成一团
扔进纸筐
这时，纸筐里慢慢传来
刚刚说的那句话
我弯下腰，从纸筐里
把那张旧纸拿出来
撕了个粉碎
就在我把碎纸片扔出去的时候
那个人在碎里
又跟我说了一句话
兄弟，你看见过碎吗
你能把旧撕成碎吗
你能把碎撕成碎吗

2000年2月2日于办公室
2000年2月20日于书房

In Pieces

Deep in the night
From an old sheet of paper
I heard words spoken, older than that paper
I walked over to the table
Leaned over the sheet of paper
Looked at it this way and that
No words from the man in the paper
Not even the grandfather of his words
Was being spoken
I crumpled the paper roughly
Threw it in the waste can
Then heard that same sentence
Calling out from the wastepaper
I bent over, pulled that paper ball
Out of the waste can
Tore it into little pieces
No sooner had I thrown them back
Than that man in the pieces
Said something more to me
What do you know about being in pieces?
Can you tear what's old into pieces?
Can you tear pieces into pieces?

2000/02/2
2000/02/20

原来

什么时候
挎上原来的那只原来的小筐
到最原来的地方
捡回最原来的事情

按原来的动作
原来的想法
还原出原来的意思
让一切一切
触及原来
到原来那里去

1985.3

Back Then

When can it happen?
I'll shoulder that basket from back then
And go where I used to back then
Pick up my doings from back then

According to my movements back then
A way of thinking from back then
Back to the point of things back then
Let everything and its brother
Get a touch of back then
By finding the way to back then

1985/3

本真

木匠
把门钉在墙上
躲在另一种门的门后
看从门里走出来的
人口和制度

门,使我们相识

1986.2

Core Identity

A carpenter
Nails a doorframe into a wall
Then watches the populace and its establishment
Go walking out the door

1986/2

一年来的借

一月份
你跟我借
磁带里的一首苏联歌曲
你说最好把列宁的言谈举止也借给你
二月份
你跟我借
刚刚收到的一笔稿费
你说最好把我的写作也借给你
三月份
你跟我借
早上送来的那份报纸
你说能否把布什和萨打姆打架的姿势也借给你
四月份
你跟我借
妻子的那件披肩
你说能否把爱情也借给你
五月份
你跟我借
余秋雨的《文化苦旅》
你说能否把他的旅程也借给你
六月份
你跟我借
经常穿用的那双布鞋
你说能否把道路也借给你
七月份
你跟我借
存放在冰箱里的那瓶酒
你说能否把醉一块借给你
八月份
你跟我借
爷爷留下来的那块老怀表
你说最好把留下来的老时光一同借给你
九月份
你跟我借
家里的那部电话
你说能否把电话里的另一端也借给你

A Year's Worth Of Borrowing

January
You want to borrow
A song on tape from the Soviet Union
And say I might as well lend you Lenin's gestures and speaking style too
February
You want to borrow
The royalty payment I just received
And say I might as well lend you my ordeal of writing
March
You want to borrow the morning paper at my door
And say how about lending you
The fighting postures of Bush and Hussein too
April
You want to borrow
The shawl my wife wears
And say how about lending you love while I'm at it
In the month of May
You want to borrow
A Bitter Journey Through Culture by Yu Qiuy
And say how about lending me his itinerary too
June
You want to borrow
The pair of cloth shoes I often wear
And say how about lending you the road as well
July
You want to borrow
The bottle of booze I keep in the fridge
And say how about lending you my drunkenness too
August
You want to borrow
The railroad watch my grandfather left me
And say how about lending you the good old days too
September
You want to borrow
The telephone in my house
And how about lending you the other end of the phone line too

十月份
你跟我借
故乡派人送来的秋天水果
你说能否把故和故乡也借给你
十一月份
你跟我借
家里惟一的那把木椅
你说最好连疲劳一块借给你
十二月份
年终岁尾
家里被你借得空空荡荡
除了我
还有什么可以借给你

2003年3月2日

October
You want to borrow
The basket of fruit someone sent from my hometown
You say how about lending you my hometown too
November
You want to borrow
The only wooden chair in my home
You say I might as well lend you my fatigue as well
December
At the tail end of the year
My home is down to the bare walls
Aside from me what is there
That I can still lend to you

2003/03/2

路过医学院门口的一次写作

疾病从X光的底片上
把学历递过来
学历在床边
劝说着死亡

死亡。谁的死亡

病情死死地盯着
医学的前方
大夫拿来一支体温计
放在我们往事的腋下
测你我友情的温度

友情。谁的友情

你躺在被英文缩写的病历里
慢的一种到来
由此，一种被翻译过来的悲伤
正慢慢向我靠拢

慢。谁的慢

2004年1月29日

Written While Passing the Gate of a Medical School

Out of the film of an X-ray
Sickness yields up a grade transcript
The transcript at death's bedside
Speaks comforting words

To death. Whose death?

A terminal condition stares rigidly
At the space ahead of medicine
A doctor brings a thermometer
For the underarm of times gone by
To test our friendship's temperature

Friendship. Whose friendship?

There you lie in a medical record
Abbreviated by English
The slow kind catches up to you

Whereupon a certain sorrow translated from English
Slowly draws near to me

Slowness. Whose slowness?

2004/1/29

抽屉里的写作

小时候
对抽屉有一种特殊的神秘感
比如糖，比如饼干
比如钱， 比如粮票
比如印在糖纸上的"最高指示"
比如烘烤在饼干上
却比饼干还要挨得更近的
穷和饿在童年里的相互停顿
统统锁在那里

抽屉
又常常是放手枪的地方
比如手枪里的电影
或是电影里的手枪
都没离开过抽屉
抽屉里的手枪
大多不是为了自卫
而是用于自杀
自杀为何选择在抽屉里？
据说，持机密者的死
亦属国家机密

长大以后
我也有了自己的抽屉
可抽屉里
除了放几粒药片
铅笔，稿纸
和用于护理远方友情的地址
别的什么也没有

不久前
我偷偷地买了一把玩具手枪
放在了抽屉里
试想着
自杀给死亡
带来了什么样的保证

Writings in a Drawer

When I was little
A drawer seemed charged with special mystery
For instance candy, or biscuits
For instance money, or ration coupons
For instance a "supreme directive" printed on a candy wrapper
For instance poverty and hunger
Baked into the biscuits
Fused and hard to dislodge from my childhood
Closer to me than the biscuits themselves
Such things were locked in a drawer

A drawer
Was often a place to keep a pistol
For instance the pistol in a movie
Or the movie within a pistol
Were never separate from the drawer
And the pistol in the drawer
Was mostly not for self-defense
But used to commit suicide
And why was a drawer the choice for suicide?
They say the death of someone privy to state secrets
Is also a state secret

Now that I'm grown up
I have a drawer of my own
But inside it, aside from a few pills
Some pencils and ruled paper
Addresses for nursing
The health of distant friendships
There is nothing at all

Not long ago I bought a toy pistol
Which I secretly put in my drawer
Trying the thought on for size
What kind of guarantee suicide would be
When it comes to death?

力量
————献给乖乖

我认为
力量是被左手损坏的
你说
右手里的力量
足可以把埋在乡下里的节日
挖掘出来
供城里人隐蔽忧伤
甚至可以把蜡烛经营夜色的时候
在乡下欠下的光芒
用民间艺术带回到城里
拿一面镜子里面的万家灯火
把债务还掉

一个来修理节日的神认为
大多数的力量在工人们那里
他们炼出了铁之后
使力量变得越来越沉
提高了天才手里的真理的分量
加快了邪恶溜进废墟的速度
另一部分力量在农民的手里
自从他们的力量
解开了农业的上衣纽扣
玉米便伸出大拇指表扬秋天
使我们突然知道该如何用筷子竖起荣耀
又知道该怎样在抚养食品的时候
去抚养我们的内心
抚养我们的种种打算

你认为
我的双手像用完的牙膏
一点力量也挤不到这张桌面上
和你较量
甚至连讲一个传说
和传说里的孩子上当受骗以后
大声哭喊的力量也没有
即使能挤出一个富翁来不及咽下去的幽默

Power
       —*for Guai Guai*

I believe
Power is undermined by the left hand
You say
The right-handed power
Is enough to dig up a country holiday
That was buried in the ground
For city people to conceal their melancholy
It can even use folk art to bring
The light-rays that were owed
When a candle tried to manage a country night
Then use the lamps of human habitation in a mirror
To repay a debt

A deity that came to repair the festival
Believes that most of the power lies with the workers
Once they smelted iron
Power took on more weight
Raising the substance of truth in the hands of genius
And hastening the speed of evil sneaking into ruins
Another portion of power lies in the hands of peasants
And since their power
Unfastened the blouse of agriculture
Ears of corn stuck out their thumbs in praise of autumn
Suddenly letting us know how honor is upheld with chopsticks
And how to care for our inner hearts
And our various intentions
As we care for our stomach's satisfaction

In your eyes
My two hands are flat like a tube of toothpaste
Unable to squeeze any power to rival you
Onto this table surface
Lacking even the power to tell a legend
Or the children deceived in the legend
Who don't even have power to wail
Even if I catch myself squeezing out a rich man's humor

也无法找一个更虚荣的场合
悄悄地打开幽默的库房
由幽默掩护我从贫困越狱
我说
如果我握住了你的手
并摸到了你的力量
那力量我可以用吗

2002．2．6农历初三于书房

I cannot find an occasion of greater vanity
To open the storehouse of humor secretly
And cover up my escape from poverty's prison
And so
If I grasp your hand
And feel your power
Can I use that power?

2002/02/6

必须

有些东西必须熟练地放在地上
比如回家的路
又比如每天派出寻找
在中文里毒死父亲早期眼泪的那句成语的脚印
和上交给母亲的身影
有些东西必须定期放在树上
比如风暴
比如被风撕下来的内心景色
有些东西必须放在一种梦里
比如再次乘坐外婆的歌谣
以及与歌谣里的恩人重逢
有些东西必须放在纸上
比如七岁下课时的骄傲
比如活在词里的外公病情
有些东西必须放在花园里
比如碑文里伟人的内心活动
有些东西必须放在石头里
比如锤子从石头的中央
拿回来的天堂上面的声音
有些东西必须放在刚刚死去的药片里
比如旧伤口和伤口里最新的凶手指纹
有些东西必须放在皮箱里
比如手段
有些东西必须放在杯子里
比如快要流不动的河流
和已经不流的友谊
有些东西必须放在楼梯里
比如无产阶级和资产阶级
有些东西必须放在爱里
比如心
有些东西必须放在天空里
比如太阳和太阳倒出来的光芒
又比如会飞的鸟
和鸟儿为了教你远离坏蛋而完成的后一种
飞翔

1999.12.24于北京平安夜

NEED

Some things need to be put on the ground skillfully
For instance the homeward road
Also for instance the footprint
Of the cliché that poisoned my father's youthful tears
Within the Chinese language
Also the receding shape I offered up to my mother
Some things need to be put up in a tree regularly
For instance a storm
Also for instance the inner scene
That was torn down by the wind
Some things need to be put into a dream
For instance once again riding on grandmother's song
And meeting my benefactor in that song
Some things need to be put on paper
For instance pride when getting out of class at age seven
For instance grandfather's sickness that lives in a word
Some things must be put in a garden
For instance the inner life of great men inscribed on plaques
Some things need to be put in a stone
For instance the sounds of heaven
Hammered back out of a stone's center
Some things need to be put into an outdated cure
For instance an old wound, and in it, a murderer's newest fingerprint
Some things need to be put in a suitcase
For instance the means to an end
Some things must be put in a cup
For instance a river that almost stopped flowing
And friendship that flows no more
Some things need to be put on a staircase
For instance the proletariat and the bourgeoisie
Some things need to be put within love
For instance the heart
Some things need to be put in the sky
For instance the sun, and rays that pour from the sun
Also birds that are able to fly
And the latter-day flight they use
That shows you how to keep distance from evil men

1993/12/24

鱼

鱼在画里
画挂在鱼的目光上
鱼，张开着的嘴
咬住我的内心活动

鱼跟我说
把水拿过来
我就能游回去
即使是眼泪

2004年2月25日

A Fish

A fish is in a painting
The painting is caught in its gaze
The fish's mouth is gulping
Biting my inner life

The fish says to me
Bring me some water
To let me swim back
Even if it is tears

2004/2/25

布艺

一块布
拦住一个季节

做这件布衣的人
是位山东老太太
她把穿这件衣裳的人的品质
缝进衣领之后
就匆匆地走了

她留下来的东西
像布艺上的针线
细而绵长
你无法知道从哪儿开始
又将在哪儿结束

2003年2月19日

Needlecraft

A piece of cloth
Wraps up a season

The one who fashioned it
Is an old woman from Shandong
Who sewed strength of character
Into the collar you would wear
Then all of a sudden went away

What remains when she is gone
Resembles the stitching of a garment
A finely drawn-out line
You cannot know where it begins
And where it is going to end

2003/02/19

直觉场

从一个时候以来
世界陆续停电
光明无法从电线杆上爬进人间

漆黑的树下
两个永远的孩子
取出储满光辉的电池
设计种种幸福
和许多意外的微笑

据说，这样的一切
属于无用的发现

1985.

Intuitive Field

From a certain time
The world had a series of blackouts
Light from a from a telephone pole could not crawl into human space

Beneath a pitch-black tree
Two eternal children
Bring out batteries fully charged with radiance
To design various kinds of happiness
And many unexpected smiles

People say, such a thing
Amounts to a useless discovery

1985

今夜，上演悲伤

在很多次以后的一次
我似乎无法再从脸上派出笑容
看守近年来的心情
只好打开手里的书
查阅悲剧和喜剧的下落
在莎士比亚约好的人生现场里
认领了一份过期的悲伤
然后，悄悄地把自己关在外省的梦里
和投身于噩梦之外
用鲜花劝说自己内心忧伤的女孩
相遇，相逢

那时，你刚刚走进影院
与一些无怨无恨的人
被并列写进人间
你们各自的生活表情
好像在夜晚里被人动过
影片里的人间
没有爷爷用过的生活
男女主角的几句主要台词
不会这么快给你们带来这么多的好处
也不可能在这一次黑暗里
把好日子换给你
电影里的话语容易生病
你们不会一下子
掏出自己的手相
在如今的这个世界上交换心意
夹在外祖母孤独里的那张电影票
是你有意放在那儿的
这样，从那天夜里
她期待一回电影
能拍摄到她的悲伤
能提前把她的悲伤演完

你确实不知道
电影究竟该如何演好我们的一生

This Evening's Feature Will Be Sorrow

This time after so many times
I can't seem to beam out a smile
Doing guard duty over my moods
These years with a book in my hand
Time to learn how tragedy and comedy turn out
On the scene of life, as embraced by Shakespeare
I'll claim a portion of outdated sorrow
Close myself in an outlander's dream
Resort to something outside of nightmare
A bouquet to urge the grieving girl in my heart
Go out to meet, encounter . . .

By then you have walked into a cinema
With people who bear you no grievance
Placed in rows and written into the crowd
The lived expressions on each of your faces
Were seemingly tampered with overnight
The human scene in the film
Not what your grandfather got out of life
The dialogue of male and female leads
Brings you no immediate benefit
The cover of this darkness gives
No quick change to better days
Speech in the film can easily get sick
You and the rest, in this kind of world
Will not be laying open your palms
To read the exchange of intentions

Your grandmother in her loneliness kept a ticket stub
From that first movie she saw
Which you have a special place for
She looked forward to another
A movie that would depict her sorrow
Perform its ending ahead of time

You don't know for certain
How movies can get it right, this performance of our life

总之，你想截住影片中
那辆运载过和平也运载过战争的西方汽车
从艺术里开出来
拖走跟在儿童身后的苦难
把哭声从生活里运走
电影演到祖国的痛苦不够的时候
世界，突然停电了
停止你把黯淡下来的日子
涂上外地的光芒
并禁止在原有的脸庞
展览忧伤
后来，你从失败的成就里退下来
可爱地坐在工业的某一个门口
看一个孩子
跟随树上醒来的果实
在树下一遍一遍地成熟

现在，我只想用橡皮
把自己一行一行地从黑暗里擦去
之后，从一棵高大的树上
沉重地滑落

1987.12.

But in this movie you want to intercept the Western truck
That has transported peace at times, and sometimes war
And drive it into the open space of art
To drag away hardship that dogged a child's footsteps
To haul the sounds of sobbing out of life
When the film shows the motherland running low on misery
The world has a sudden power failure
This stops you from painting the outland's brightness
Over days grown gloomy
Forbidden now are exhibitions of grief
On your face as it was originally intended
Later, you step down from the achievement of defeat
And sit loveably in a doorway of industrialization
You watch a child beneath a tree
Along with each fruit that wakens in its branches
He ripens again and again

Right now, I wish to use an eraser
To rub myself out of darkness line by line
And then, from up in a tall tree
Drop down with all my weight

1987/12

桌子上的内心活动

当我通过镜子的反光
区分父亲和母亲的时候
当邻居家的万鹏姐姐
用一个纸叠出来的下午
使我把身上的友谊全部输掉的时候
便围着桌子
开始了由小到大的生活

小的时候
常常把桌子当作玩具
有时把它当成国家地理
顺着木纹里的道路
在山川田野走来走去
即可走完这一生
有时把它当作剧场的舞台
自己亲自扮演一位开明皇帝
每天一千次地把手臂伸给贫民百姓
让他们顺着政权从生活的底层爬上来
之后，取消零度以下的生活
之后，把汉语发到每一个人的手上
乃至我剩下的最后一份好心情
也发给他们
并亲自给这一代人民
洗衣服，甚至擦地板
允许他们的多年往事抵押给国家
剧情的途中
母亲下班回家
倾刻间，知道了什么叫垂帘听政
有时，把母亲出嫁用过的那块红布
盖在桌子的上面
它便成了家里的太阳
从此，认为布里也有光芒

晚饭的时候
我的很多来自于桌子上的内心活动
被母亲切菜时的菜刀

Inner Life at the Table

Across from my parents I took to mirror gazing
As I noticed their different expressions
And once I yielded every ounce of friendship
To Wanpeng the older girl from next door
For an afternoon of folding paper
That was the beginning, around that table
Of life that goes from small to large

When I was small
I often treated the table as a toy
At times it sufficed as a nation's geography
The roads along its grain
Were terrain where I walked back and forth
So much did I trust the stride of those years
Thinking that to walk back and forth
Would get me through my entire life
Sometimes I made it the stage of a theater
Took for myself the enlightened ruler's role
A thousand times a day reaching toward poor people
Letting them climb from life's bottom layer
In line with my regime
Later, I would dispense with life below zero
I would hand out the Chinese language to all
Until the last good mood remaining to me
Would revert to them
Also, for citizens of this era
I personally did the laundry, even cleaned the floor
As soon as mother got off work I knew
What it was to govern from behind a curtain
Sometimes I covered the table
With red cloth from my mother's wedding
Turning it into a sun within our home
Giving me the notion that cloth holds rays of light

At dinner time my inner life at that table
Was cut through by penetrating gleams
Not concealed by my mother's vegetable knife

泄露出的锋芒劈成两半
一半成为泪水被桌腿挽留成另外一种力量
另一半成为我后来的内幕

长大以后
我依旧带领着这张桌子生活
不过桌上摆放的不再是碗筷和菜粥
而是白纸、铅笔和水杯
几乎是在天黑之前
外地的词语
要长期住在每一张纸上
外省的地方方言
要通过铅笔的血统变成汉语的最后一次喷嚏

桌上杯子里的水
随时都可能成为我去向的河流

1999.12.26.于家中

Half was held back as tears by the table leg
To become another kind of strength
Half became my hidden side

Grown to adulthood
I bring the old table along in life
But no longer set it with chopsticks and bowls
Now it's blank paper, pen and glass of water
Almost before nightfall
Words from other places settle down on every sheet
Dialect from other provinces
Has to come through the bloodline of a pencil
To become the final sneeze
Of our Sinitic tongue.

Water in a cup on the table
At any time may become a stream
That will bear me along

1999/12/26

麦城：一九八八年孤独成果

有人在世纪末的最后一处苦难现场里
抓紧给自己写信
从汉语里寻找借口去报答自己
而且凡动用外祖父内心里的话语
便迅速给自己编造众多的绝密罪恶
二十五分钟之内实行自杀
为有这样一种他人无法跟踪的失望
他决心于今天夜里按原计划激动
并借来电视转播出来的哀愁
加强孤独效果
在街心湖畔的河岸上
用鱼竿指出从前掉进深渊的童年
和不该从孩子的眼睛里
抬出来的蹉跎岁月
让每支香烟都能燃烧出唯心主义
作为写信的特别纪律
无论有害或无害的语言
全部送往医院进行美学治疗
以确保每封信寄出日期的美丽
他决心把信一直写到
所有的坟墓里住满值得大笑的孤独
和褪色的野心
给每一间坟墓
重新换上不锈钢棺材
避免悼词生锈
对坟墓里的部分同志
公开进行违法乱纪考试
允许他们委托他人在人间悔恨
然后，对活下来的这些人
进行逃离死亡教育
使他们服从粮食生长的需要

他深信可以把每一封信
写得让所有人看后立即严格要求自己
甚至可以使一百多个国家的现任总统
同时放松真理

Mai Cheng's Solitary Achievements of 1988

A man situated at the waning century's ultimate debacle
Seizes the time to write himself a letter
In the Sinitic tongue he finds pretexts to reward himself
But at each use of his grandfather's private language
He quickly frames himself with numerous crimes
And in twenty-five minutes annihilates himself
Out of disappointment not traceable by others
He resolves to pass a night of due intensity
And resorts to a mournful broadcast on TV
To enhance the lonely effects

On the riverbank of the plaza's reflecting pool
A fishing pole marks the abyss where childhood fell
And those emptily-eked-out years
That shouldn't be reeled in by child's eyes
Let each cigarette fume with idealist philosophy
And let the code of letter writing dictate
That any utterance, harmful or otherwise
Must receive aesthetic treatment in a hospital
Guaranteeing beauty on any day when a letter is sent

He vows to keep writing letters until
All graves are occupied with ridiculous solitude
And faded colors of ambition
And he will use the kind of stainless steel for coffins
That does away with need for rusty elegies
He'll expose certain comrades in their graves
For their infringement of anti-squatters' laws
At least letting them entrust regrets to the living
And then educating the survivors
On ways to keep ahead of death
By serving the needs of food crops

He trusts he can write each letter in such a way
To make readers demand more of themselves
Or even cause presidents of a hundred or more nations
To relax at the same time about truth

参加由阿拉法特召开的
环境屡遭污染的最大淡水湖——内塔尼亚湖
和平赌博会议
研究真理紧张问题
为了在纪念馆里的皇帝没订购耳机以前
他坚持把地方口音全部杀害
并且，一夜之间
取消派朦胧诗替宋词报仇的纲要
根据拖拉机身体上的一份文件
决定开展批林批孔整风运动

几天之后
他学会了坐在椅子上
面对伟人的死整夜整夜地愤怒
和大笔大笔地占用古人的忧伤
包括用红色的巴黎公社铅笔
批改苏联的遗嘱工作
学会了给世界各国的强盗
打长途电话
告诉他们香港返回中国的日期
日期放在他站起来的骨骼里
（偷走这样的日期太难，太累）
蚊子们总是在他的耳边嘀嘀咕咕
说他的耳朵里有洪水灾害
使他无法参加最后一场国际睡眠决赛
也无法鼓励涂口红的玩具们
去投靠永恒的爱情
于是，每天的早晨
他开始把汉语从家里搬出来
一字一句地放在人间里
请大家读一读官府里的事
用从未洗过的黑色发丝
接通遥远的西方光辉
照耀眼下的这点人生
然后，提起墙角的痰桶
把病句倒掉

信写到半路的时候
世界突然开始回收汉字
同时征收写作里的状态

Maybe even join a conference convened by Arafat
To gamble for peace at Lake Neitaniya
The biggest freshwater lake, now badly polluted
They will do studies on the tension of truth
For the emperor in his mausoleum who hasn't ordered headphones
Who insisted on stamping out local accents
And in a single night cancelled the memorandum
That would have Misty poets avenge Sung dynasty lyrics
Preferring to launch a campaign against Confucius
Based on a directive from the body of a tractor

After a few days of this
He mastered the trick of sitting in a chair
Seething at grand old death the whole night long
With big pen strokes co-opting sorrows of ancients
To the point of using a red pen from the Paris Commune
To mark changes of assignment in the Soviet Union's last testament
He learned to phone robbers all over the world
To give reminders of Hong Kong's handover date
A date with a place in his now-erect bone structure
(To steal that date would bring a great deal of trouble)

Mosquitoes with their constant hum and whine
Spoke of a flood that would engulf his ears
Keeping him from international sleeping events
And ending his assurances to lipstick-wearing toys
That lasting love could be their refuge
He began moving the Sinitic tongue out of his house
Word by word he placed it in the social realm
Inviting all to read what happens in officialdom
He used unwashed black hair for a filament
Connected to brilliance from the distant West
To illumine his own little patch of human life
Then picked up the spittoon in the corner
And disposed of fallacy-stricken sayings

Halfway along in his writing of letters
The world started recycling Sinitic characters
And recruiting the state of mind he was writing in

没办法,他只好跑到一所医学仓库
找来一千种名人病历
护理生存观念
经过长期的自我忧患意识磨练
国际精神分裂主义联盟
批准他为最佳职业病人
后来,传说他写的其中一封信
被收入大不列颠百科全书的最后一卷

1988.3.
1998.12.

Unable to help himself, he ransacked medical records
And dug up a thousand famous case histories
He nursed the ills of ideas about survival
After a long toughening process of dread and concern
The International League of Psychosis
Named him the finest professional patient
Later, some say one of his letters was included
In the ultimate volume of the Encyclopedia Britannica

1988/3
1998/12

视觉广场

关上那扇旧门
门上好像爬满了历代的敲门声
夜,一点一点地涂掉墙上的一句诺言
鸟儿的奇迹被绑在窗前的一棵树上
在胡同的拐角
有人被一群黑暗堵住
另一部分新的黑暗也蹲在那里
我想这个时候
不会有谁高尚地举起遥远的鲜花
站在没有噩梦的某一个门口
去相信有一种来临

听说你已经绕过儒家的哲学
正存在主义地从通俗唱法的路上走来
最后走成最有希望敲门的人
凭着生动的美味咳嗽
我再次坐在椅子上
掂量如今剩下的几句话语
今后分几次感人
想一些康德一直忽视的某些小事

现在,城里几乎无人点亮灯光
向我提供一块可读的晚间人生
只好沉重地抓起甜蜜的电话
电话却还是没有安装
全体女孩疲于热爱我的题目
和逃往祖国的句子
在无轨电车
没有正确地把你的生活运来以前
我不太自豪地重新拎起古老的酒壶
到处几滴可怜的西方的格言
或者咬一口酸味的水果
为窗外那个被呼唤的孩子忧伤

桌上那支摔裂的铅笔
无法叙述风暴欠下的一笔笔伤痕

The Plaza of Eyesight

Pull the old door closed
It seems to crawl with knocking down through the ages
Night, bit by bit erases a promise on the wall
Miracle of birds snared in a tree before the window
Where the alley makes a blind turn
A band of dark ones closes in on someone
The new part of darkness hunkers off to one side
At times like this I do not believe
Anyone will stand in a doorway free of nightmares
High-mindedly holding flowers toward the sky
In the name of some kind of advent

They say you've made a detour past Confucian philosophy
And you approach existentially on a road of pop vocals
Trekking made you the most likely one to knock on doors
On the strength of a deeply savored cough
I settle back into a chair
Trying the heft of the sentences left to me
The right apportionment to move someone
Thinking of trivia persistently ignored by Kant
Few city dwellers use one lamp's illumination
Right now life does not give me a readable evening
What else but heavily to pick up a sweet telephone
The one I keep trying to install
The ranks of young womanhood have their hands full
Just loving my titles, my lines that flee to the motherland
Until the trackless trolley that transports you
Can get your life here more fittingly
Abashedly again I raise this old decanter
To pour out Western proverbs in pitiful drops
Or bite into a sour apple
And feel sorry for the child outside my window
Whom someone is calling to

The fountain pen on my desk, split from being thrown
Cannot narrate scars left owing by the storm

你可以从那本没合上的书里
去一行一行地数一遍
还有多少现成的真理值得我们不去说遍所有的诺言
面对墙上的镜子
你也可以亲自鼓励对自己微笑
甚至可以想入非非
当然，你早晚要从镜子里下来
一笔一画地做一次人民

你用早期的目光
向我推荐筹建法律的远方
我说你离开哪里
哪里就成为你的远方
当我们一同走过一个地方
就有人随后赶到那里
无法恢复原状地为我们痛哭
也许，我们成年成年地抬着苦难的生活
在世界上走得太久太久
其实，世界的道路很宽很宽
足够我们的脚步一次走完所有的离别
又一次走向无数个闪耀的重逢
那么，根本没有伟大的必要
在一条路上我们悲痛万分地相识
一次性地说尽人间的千言万语
然后，每个人的脸上
去轮流展览几代人的尴尬

以后，我用孩子的蜡笔
涂画了一条近路离开了那个夜晚
直到不能怀念和想象
剩下一片粗糙的敲门声
在那扇门上

1987.9.

An open book on the desk, count out line by line
So much ready-to-hand truth makes it important
Not to utter every single promise
Facing the mirror on the wall
Encourage the smiles you give yourself
Or go down avenues of thought
Sometime you'll have to come down from the mirror
And take pains to make your mark as citizen

Using the gaze of your early days
You recommend the distance for formulating laws
I say that wherever you depart from
Becomes the place distant from you
When we pass over a place in this world together
Someone arrives there behind us
And does the sobbing for us, unrestorably
Perhaps it has been too long
Year after year carrying this tough life around with us
Enough to pace out our leavetaking all at once
At once striding again toward countless shining reunions
That being so, there is no need for greatness
We know each other agonizingly on the road
At once we utter what there is to say of this reality
And then all of our faces
Take turns displaying chagrin of various eras

Afterwards, with a child's crayon
I draw an approach by which I depart this dark night
Past recollecting or imagining
All that remains is the sound of rough knocking
On the outside of that same door

1987/9

在困惑里接待生活

A
门在墙上活下来
墙死于墙体的深处

门敞开语言
语言挡住你做人的几种迹象
从那扇门里
你发现婚姻还在活着
同时，发现一直延长到
孩子不止一次用门里的哭声
给你带路

敲门的动机
总落入猎手的恐惧里
门正面形容你
你却反面理解了我
在另一种门的门后
你把已经松开一年多的手
再次握成凶器
与阴谋相处
你又成了我们的门

门，或许就是阴谋

B
桌上的杯子
总提起口渴的事
端起杯子
却不见你爬上岸来
杯子里，打不出水井

C
大约深夜一点
疾病使帝王的想象陷入绝境
当朝神医缝合好
奄奄一息的江山落日
后，前往鲁班的家中
把岁月锯成一副担架

In Bewilderment, Playing the Host to Life

A
The door in the wall stays alive
The wall dies in its own deep structure

The door opens up to language
Language blocks certain marks of your humanity
Though the doorway
You discover that marriage is still alive
As you discover it can keep going
Time and again, if only a child shows the way
With sounds of crying.

The motive for knocking on a door
Boils down to the fear of a hunter
The door casts you in a flattering light
Yet you view me from my worst side
Behind another kind of door
The grasp of your hand that softened for a year
Tightens as if around a weapon
And plotting keeps you company.
By now you are the door for both of us,

A door, perhaps, is nothing but a plot.

B
The cups on the table
Keep reminding me of thirst
I hold up my glass
But do not see you climbing to the bank.
A glass is no place for digging a well.

C
Deep in the night, at one o'clock or thereabouts
Sickness steers a ruler's musings into a corner.
The most gifted doctor in the current dynasty
Sews up the waning days of our patrimony
Then in the workshop of a mythical carpenter
Saws the passing years into a shoulder pole

从帝王的病情里
把荣华富贵抬出来
京剧里的先帝
没从乐谱里拉出最好的情感
为社稷伴奏
苦难被二胡念出声来

好不容易
跪在皇妃的死亡里
悲痛的表情
又如何从穷人的内心掏出来

D
道路，纷纷逃往一双布鞋
鞋，一步使我迈进真理

E
一部电影里的天气太冷
冷得无法从忧伤里支付笑容
翻开手里的书
李白的诗正在去往四川的路上
蜀道两侧被风刮倒的岁月
使李白决定把一首长诗种在四川
日后长成一棵大树
结满五言七律
或者让它长成一块巨石
镇风祛寒
掖在李白腰间的那个酒壶
装着"蜀道之难，难于上青天
使人听此凋朱颜"的人生句式
我真想上前摘下那壶酒
把他的豪言壮志倒在我的碗里
把李白剩下来的才气喝干
由我来感动我的后半生

F
已经是后一种死亡比喻
迫使我摆出好兵帅克形象
并掏出把一个二战英雄的名字送进天堂的老枪

From the ruler's pathology
He carries out loads of excess
The previous ruler in our current opera
Could not catch the spirit behind the notes
To serenade our beleaguered land
Misery is uttered on two strings of an erhu

It was not easy to find ourselves on our knees
Under the pall of an empress' death
And how were these grieving expressions
Pulled out from a poor man's hollow heart?

D
A swarm of roads flees into a pair of cloth shoes
One step, and we stride into the truth.

E
The weather in a movie is too cold
My sorrow is too cold to summon up smiles
As I leaf through the book in my hand
Li Bai's poems make a trek to Sichuan
Blown-over years along the steep road
Have him wishing to plant a big poem on arrival
Later it will put forth long branches
At their tips will grow quatrains and octaves
Or maybe he'll plant a great boulder
The kind that stabilizes weather
The gourd full of wine tied at his waist
Holds those sentences that nailed down life's ordeals:
"Hard is the road to Shu
  harder than reaching the blue sky
  Only to hear of it
  Makes young faces wither and dry"
Let me snatch that gourd from his waist
And drain Li Bai's talent to the dregs
So the second half of my life
Will be moved by what I write

F
It's already a late kind of metaphor for death
Driving me into a guise of gallant command

瞄准女人的情怀
击落一地爱情

G
男人在词典里造句
女孩拧松句子里的语法
一个字押着下一个词
嘴商量着幽默的出发时间

H
多想给痛苦安上嘴唇
让他说出凶手的长相
然后，再陪你慢慢地疼

I
是谁命令夜色
从烛光上爬过去的
又是谁把我们的友情
分开放着的

J
小道消息
你想在一千九百八十八页
第十行再次编造我
而我在一千九百八十七页
第九行的时候
悄悄地逃出了你的构思

据说，有人把那一页
从岁月的脸上撕下来
扔在小孩的谎话里
结果，你自己
最先掉进了现代悲剧

K
悼词出卖死亡技巧
终于，你还是死于肉体

1988.10. / 1998.12

I pull out a weapon made divine by a hero's name
Aim it at a woman's soft center
And bag myself a swath of affection

G
A man riffles for sentences in a dictionary
A woman unscrews the strings of grammar
A word coerces a phrase to march along
The mouth considers when to issue humor

H
Oh if I could install a mouth on this pain
Let it speak of the killer's countenance
While I take my time aching in your company

I
Who commanded the dark night
To pass over the candle light?
And who placed our friendship
In this place and that?

J
So says the rumor mill
In the 10th line of the 1988th page
You wish to re-edit me
But by the 9th line of the 1987th page
I give your intentions the slip

It has been said
Someone tore that page
From the face of a passing year
And threw it into a childish lie
It turns out, you were the first
To be claimed by that modern tragedy

K
Elegies capitalize on techniques of dying
But in the end, you die of the body

1988/10; 1998/12

歌剧里的圈套

从节目单上往下看
歌剧里
还剩下一把椅子
我试着把它搬出来
搬到喉咙和歌声的夹层里去

我转到歌剧的身后
印在节目单上的人
正向场内的黑暗鞠着躬
涂在今夜纸上的表情
比幕布还宽

歌剧使劲地扯着
我的耳朵
高音C
掏出来的这一夜伤悲
使人无法入睡

此时的剧场
比歌剧还小
坐在台下的婚姻
正成为歌剧的难度
爱和被爱
同时被罚出场外

歌剧用东方人的命运
开的头
歌声，从西方飞回来
又飞了回去
台词，却被扣在东方受审

演出快要结束时
我看见歌剧里的泪水
正往台下流
慌忙之中，我向后退去
退回到自己的眼睛为止

2003.3.21

An Operatic Intrigue

Looking down from the program notes
At the only chair left
Belonging to this opera
I attempt to move it away
Move it away from here
To the interstice between throat and song

I go round to the opera's backside
As the person printed in the program notes
Bows to the darkest row of seats
An expression wider than any curtain
Is painted on the paper of evening

The opera pummels my eardrums
Its high C
Reaches into my ears
It drags out this night's sorrow
And won't let me sleep

The amphitheater of this moment
Does not measure up to the opera
The marriage sitting before the stage
Is what makes the opera difficult
Loving and being loved, at once
Are banned from the hall

The dramatic tension is premised
On the fate of oriental people
Singing voices fly in from the West
Then fly back, but lyrics
Are detained in the East for questioning

As the performance nears its conclusion
I see tears from the opera
Flowing toward the seats
In a rush I draw away
But go no further than my eyes

2003.3.21

www.ingramcontent.com/pod-product-compliance
Lightning Source LLC
Chambersburg PA
CBHW021327190426
43193CB00039B/335